CROATIA

UNPACKED

Susie Brooks

WAYLAND

www.waylandbooks.co.uk

Published in paperback in 2017 by Wayland
Copyright © Wayland, 2017

Editor: Nicola Edwards
Designer: Peter Clayman
Cover design: Matthew Kelly

Dewey number: 949.7'203-dc23
ISBN: 978 0 7502 9165 1
10 9 8 7 6 5 4 3 2 1

Wayland, an imprint of
Hachette Children's Group
Part of Hodder and Stoughton
Carmelite House
50 Victoria Embankment
London EC4Y 0DZ

An Hachette UK Company
www.hachette.co.uk
www.hachettechildrens.co.uk

Printed and bound in China

10 9 8 7 6 5 4 3 2 1

Picture acknowledgements: All images and graphic elements courtesy of Shutterstock except:
p19 (b) Wikimedia Commons; p21 (T) Corbis.com

Every attempt has been made to clear copyright. Should there be any inadvertent omission,
please apply to the publisher for rectification.

Contents

Croatia: Unpacked

Welcome to Croatia, one of Europe's top holiday hotspots! It's a land of picturesque towns perched by crystal-clear seas, with hundreds of off-the-beaten-track islands. You can join beach-loving crowds or get away into unspoilt countryside – just look out for bears and wolves. Have a go at sailing, hiking, skiing... or watch Croatians play the sport they love best, football! People really are rushing to Croatia, so let's unpack and see why.

Fact File

Area: 56,594 sq km
Population: 4,470,534 (July 2014)
Capital city: Zagreb
Land borders: 2,237km with five countries
Currency: Croatian kuna
Main language: Croatian

Flag:

Croatia

You can see on this map how Croatia shares land borders with five other countries. Croatia's capital city, Zagreb, is shown too, along with some of the other places you will discover in this book.

Austria

Italy

Slovenia

Hungary

Drava

Danube

■ Zagreb

Croatia

Serbia

Sava

○ Gorjani

Rovinj ○

Sinj ○

Cres

Plitvice National Park

Bosnia and Herzegovina

Pag

Dinaric Alps

Zadar ○

Krka

Dalmatia

Adriatic Sea

Split ○

Brac

Hvar

Montenegro

Mljet ○

Dubrovnik

The hilltop town of Završje has its own leaning tower – it tilts like the famous Leaning Tower of Pisa in Italy.

Hvar Island basks in 2,700 hours of sunshine per year – that's more than Sydney, Australia!

Kaleidoscope Country

Croatia's story shows that it's a place worth fighting for! Over thousands of years, different kingdoms, empires and republics have taken charge of the land. It has been joined with Hungary, invaded by Turks, ruled in part by Italy – and that's just the start. Bombarded with such a kaleidoscope of cultures, Croatia has become a varied and intriguing country.

Early Days

It was the Romans who first named Croatia's coastal area, Dalmatia, established in 32 BCE. They ruled this and the rest of the region for centuries, building an explosion of new roads and towns. The name Croatia comes from a people called the Croats, who moved in from the 600s. Centuries of power struggles followed, with a series of different nations taking control.

Pula's amphitheatre could seat 25,000 Romans! It's still used for concerts today.

Yugoslavia

In 1918, following World War I, Croatia joined with some of its neighbours to form the Kingdom of Serbs, Croats and Slovenes. Later this became Yugoslavia. After World War II (1939-45), a leader called Tito began to rebuild Yugoslavia as a communist state. He helped to boost industry and the economy – but after his death in 1980, trouble flared up between the different ethnic groups.

A statue of Tito, who held Yugoslavia together for 35 years.

Breakaway Wars

The nations of Yugoslavia gradually broke apart, leading to conflicts including the Bosnian War (1992-95). More than 100,000 people were killed – thousands of them civilians. Serbian leaders tried to 'ethnically cleanse' Croats and Muslims from parts of the region (they were later arrested for war crimes). Croatia and its various neighbours eventually became independent states.

Croatia's population is now 90 per cent Croat, with Serbs the next biggest group.

Pay a Visit

Today, tourists are the people fighting to get to Croatia! Over 10 million travellers flock here each year to soak up the natural beauty and culture. There are more islands than you could hope to visit, buildings surviving from ancient times, and activities that could keep you un-bored for ever. Here are just a few things to tickle your tourist taste buds.

NO WAY!

Tourism in Croatia employs around 140,000 people and brought in more than 4.5 billion euros in 2013.

Walk like a Roman through the marble-clad old town of Zadar – when filmmaker Alfred Hitchcock visited he described the sunsets as the best in the world. There's an organ in Zadar that's powered by sea waves, so you can listen to music as you admire them!

Put on some walking boots and tackle the Premužic Trail – a breathtaking 57km hiking route, taking in mountain ridges, thick forests and dazzling views.

You can tell that colourful Rovinj was once ruled by Italy – many people here speak Italian, and even the street signs are bilingual! Rovinj used to be an island, but residents joined it to the mainland in the 18th century.

Take a day trip from the capital Zagreb to see Trakošćan, one of Croatia's most magical castles. These days it's a museum – you can rent a paddleboat on the lake in the grounds.

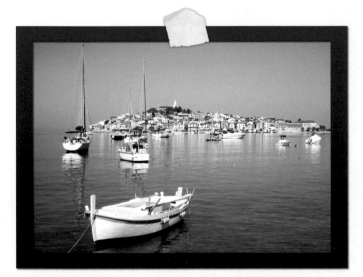

The crystal-clear waters of the Adriatic Sea are a paradise for swimming, paddling, diving, kayaking, sailing and more. Watch out for sea urchins and posh people partying on yachts.

Fancy some speleology? (That's cave study to you!) Croatia is a Karst region, a type of rocky landscape that's packed with sinkholes and caves. Wrap up warm and check out the stalactites and stalagmites in deep, dark grottos.

Sea and Snow

Imagine sledging in mountain snow, then swimming in turquoise sea all on the same day. You can do that in Croatia! The shores are lined with rugged peaks, while inland you'll find rolling hills and plains. You can hop around a staggering 1,185 islands, and take a dip in scenic lakes and rivers too. Enjoy long hours of Mediterranean sunshine, or a cooler continental climate away from the coast.

High Points

The Dinaric Alps stretch north-south across Croatia, rising up to 1,831m at their highest peak, Dinara. They're draped in thick forests, with deep gorges and caves cutting through the rock. In Dalmatia the mountains literally have their feet in the water, as they drop straight down to the coast. Up high it's cold and snowy in winter – you can ski here, less than 20km from the sea.

NO WAY!

The bura is a cold, dry wind that hits the coast of Croatia – sometimes at speeds of over 200km/h!

From ocean depths to mountain heights – Croatia has it all!

Water Features

Rivers and streams criss-cross the Croatian countryside – some even run deep underground! Pick the right spot and you can go rafting on whitewater rapids. Hikers love the Plitvice Lakes National Park, with its 16 bright blue lakes, linked by 92 waterfalls (if you're feeling lazy, visit by train or boat). The Krka river also has some famous – and deafeningly noisy – falls.

Wooden walkways take you round the Plitvice park – don't slip off!

Island Coast

If you stretched out Croatia's coastline, including its islands, it would reach further than from London to New York. There's an island here for everyone, from small banks of rock to Cres, the largest. Visit Mljet for unspoilt nature, Brac for watersports, Susak for sand or Hvar (the sunniest spot in Croatia) for celebrity spotting. The vast majority of the islands are uninhabited.

Guess why Galešnjak is known as the island of love!

Time-Travel Cities

You can take a journey through time in Croatia's cities. Buzzing with modern life, they're also home to ancient palaces, medieval castles and traditional cobblestone streets. About three in five Croatians live in urban areas, and a quarter live in the four biggest cities alone. Croatia's towns developed rapidly after World War II, leaving rural areas lagging behind.

Dubrovnik's wall wraps around the city for nearly 2km.

Adriatic Pearl

The must-see city of Dubrovnik is nicknamed the 'Pearl of the Adriatic'. Founded in the seventh century as a centre of maritime trade, it's now like a time capsule, packed with medieval architecture and pedestrian alleys. Surrounding this fairytale scene is a mighty defensive wall. You can walk along the top of it and see why the city was used as a setting for the fantasy TV series *Game of Thrones*!

Fit for an Emperor

In Croatia's second-largest city, Split, you can step into Roman Emperor Diocletian's palace. No expense was spared in building it – there are even sphinxes imported from Egypt. Created at the turn of the fourth century and modified in the Middle Ages, it's now more like a town in itself. You can explore the marble walkways, ancient ruins and modern shops and cafés on an organized tour.

Check out Emperor Diocletian's retirement home!

NO WAY!

Hum, in the region of Istria, claims to be the world's smallest town. Barely 20 people live there at any one time!

Capital Charm

About one million people live in Croatia's lively capital, Zagreb. The city's name means 'behind the hill' – it lies at the foot of Mount Medvednica, a short tram-ride away. Zagreb was founded in 1094 and still keeps its olden-day charm. At the same time, it's a hotbed of modern arts, culture and industry. The quietest time to come is in summer, when people head for the coast to escape the heat.

Zagreb combines history with cutting-edge culture.

Country Quiet

I t's hard to imagine life beyond Croatia's happening cities and tourist-packed coast, but for many Croatians, sleepy rural villages are still home. Farming and fishing are traditional activities here, and production of wine and olives is now booming. Depending on where you are in the country, you'll also find fields of sugar beet, cereals, sunflowers, lavender, and endless vegetables and fruits.

Excellent Olives

Many Croatian families make their own olive oil, and it's produced on a commercial scale too. The region of Istria is known for its high-quality extra virgin olive oil. To get the best results, harvest time has to be just right – usually that's mid-October. Hand-picking or raking the olives from the branches stops them being bruised, before they're sent straight to an oil mill for pressing.

Croatia has about 3.5 million olive trees.

Great Grapes

They've been growing grapes here for 2,500 years, since the ancient Greeks arrived. Now Croatia makes about 60 million litres of wine each year! Many families plant small hobby vineyards, alongside hundreds of commercial wine estates. Most Croatian wine is drunk within the country, rather than being exported – but that doesn't stop local varieties winning international awards.

Hillside vineyards mean a climb at picking time.

NO WAY!

On the island of Brijuni, there's a 1,600-year-old olive tree, planted by the Romans!

Village Living

Away from Croatia's chock-a-block coast, you'll find lonely clusters of stone or timber houses. Village people grow fruits and vegetables or keep animals on their land, and many have an outdoor kitchen. Those who live on islands tend to farm or fish and chug around in their own small boats. Agritourism is on the rise, so you can experience rural life for yourself.

Whoever lives here must really like cabbage.

Playing Ball

I f the word *nogomet* means nothing to you, wait till you get to Croatia. It's what they call football, the nation's favourite sport. When the national team is playing, streets become red-and-white rivers of fans dressed in their chequered strip. Crowds gather at cafés to watch games on their terrace screens. Listen out for roars when Croatia scores, and get ready to join in the singing!

National Team

Croatia made their FIFA World Cup debut in 1998 with the tournament's top scorer, Davor Šuker, shooting them into third place. They've only failed to qualify once since. The team has slipped below the top 10 in FIFA world rankings (from 4th in 2013) but still holds the nation in hope. Captain Darijo Srna is the most-capped player in the history of the team.

Captain Srna takes a kick for Croatia.

Multi-Talented

In London 2012, Croatia won Olympic medals in sports as varied as athletics, water polo, shooting and taekwondo. They also star in handball, basketball, alpine skiing and tennis (player Marin Čilić ranks in the world top ten). *Picigin*, invented in Split, is a shallow-water game that's popular at the seaside – players have to keep a ball above the water surface, batting it around with their hands.

Čilić swipes his way to victory at the 2014 US Open.

Eternal Derby

There's an ongoing rivalry between Croatia's two leading football clubs – Dinamo Zagreb and Hajduk Split. Known as the Eternal Derby, it goes back more than 90 years. DZ have the edge, but loyal supporters on both sides go wild at every match. Several DZ stars have been sold to foreign clubs, including Luka Modrić (Real Madrid) and Mateo Kovačić (Inter Milan).

Fans support the national football team.

NO WAY!

Croatian tennis ace Goran Ivanišević won Wimbledon in 2001, after entering on a wildcard. Croatia also boasts the tallest player in the game – Ivo Karlović (6'10")!

In the Wild

Croatia may be a small country, but it's big when it comes to nature. With 19 national and nature parks, and around 38,000 known species, it is richer in plants and wildlife than many other places in Europe. Prepare to meet wolves, bears, golden eagles and more...

Croatia's brown bear is big and heavy, probably because it eats anything from fungi to fish! Despite its huge weight, it can stand up on its back legs to look out for danger or food.

The national flower, *iris croatica*, grows in hilly parts of Croatia. It's strictly protected, so don't pick it!

The lynx – Europe's biggest wildcat – will mew, hiss, purr and stalk prey just like domestic moggies! It can be found, if you look very hard, in the Dinaric Alps.

Southern festoon butterfly

The Mediterranean monk seal is one of the most endangered sea mammals in the world – it was thought to be extinct in the Adriatic Sea, but is now making a comeback.

Cleopatra, little tiger blue, southern festoon, great sooty satyr... what are they? Names of just a few of the hundreds of butterfly species found in the River Kupa valley.

Learning to fly can be risky for baby Griffon vultures on the island of Cres. They're the only vultures in the world that roost by the sea, making for some splashy crash landings.

NO WAY!

Risnjak National Park's name comes from the Croatian for lynx – *ris*.

Living in dark underground caves, the olm doesn't need good eyesight. This big, pink salamander is blind but has great hearing. What's more, it can survive for up to 10 years without food!

Being Croatian

Listen to Croatians singing their national anthem, and you'll soon see how proud they are of their country. They're also passionate and hospitable people who put their family and friends first. Working hard is important, but Croatians make the most of their leisure time too. Weekends are for family get-togethers, long lunches and playing sport, or going for walks.

Keeping Faith

Overwhelmingly a Roman Catholic country, you'll hear church bells wherever you go in Croatia. Every village and town has its own patron saint, and the Virgin Mary (or 'Gospa') is worshipped countrywide. About 4 per cent of the population (mainly Serbs) are Orthodox Christians. There are also small numbers of Muslims and Protestants.

Pilgrims visit the Marija Bistrica Catholic shrine.

Primary education is compulsory and free.

Choice of Schools

Children start school at the age of 6 or 7, usually having been to preschool. At 15, they leave elementary school and can choose to go on to a gymnasium (grammar school), a vocational school (technical, industrial or craft based) or an art school (music, dance or art). Although this secondary education isn't yet compulsory, the government is planning to change the rules.

NO WAY!

As part of the wedding tradition, families offer up a fake bride (often a man dressed in white) before the real one comes out!

Wedding Winners

'Buying the bride' is a Croatian tradition that's less like shopping than it sounds! Before a wedding, the groom – along with friends and musicians – goes to the bride's house and 'barters' with the family to marry her. Usually he manages to prove his worth through singing or strength, rather than handing over money. Once he has 'won' his wife-to-be, they go to the wedding together.

Dubrovnik's Rector Palace is a popular backdrop for wedding photos!

A Place in Europe

Croatia has had a hard time over the last 20 years and its economy has taken a battering. Many people are out of work — especially the young. In 2013, Croatia joined the European Union after a ten-year wait. People celebrated the new chapter with fireworks, fanfares and dancing. EU membership brings Croatia great opportunities, and also some big challenges.

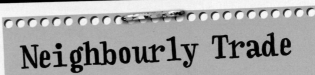

Neighbourly Trade

Croatia does almost two-thirds of its trade with EU partners — Italy, just across the sea, comes top. Its biggest exports are transport equipment, machinery, fuels and chemicals. In 2013, exports brought in around 9 million euros — though Croatia's imports cost nearly twice as much.

Brain Drain

For many young Croatians, moving abroad is the best hope for a good job. Doctors, for example, can earn up to ten times more overseas. Around 15,000 people left Croatia in 2013. The government hopes to slow this brain drain and bring talent back to Croatia.

Croatia is well placed for trade in Europe, with good roads and ports for shipping goods.

Tourist Magnet

Tourism is the jewel in Croatia's crown. It has one of Europe's fastest-growing tourist industries, with more than 12 million people arriving in 2013. Most visitors come from EU countries, Germany being the keenest. It's a race to the coast in summer months, but winter snow draws skiers too.

By 2020, Croatia plans to become one of the world's top 20 travel destinations.

NO WAY!

Croatia's currency is the kuna, named after a ferret-like animal that used to be traded for its fur.

REPUBLIKA HRVATSKA 1 KUNA

Original Inventions

Croatians have invented many things, from the necktie to the mechanical pencil! In today's tough environment, fresh ideas still shine through. Meet Rimac Concept_One, made by a Zagreb company – it's the world's first electric 'supercar'.

Concept_One reaches 100km/h in 2.8 seconds and tops 300km/h!

23

All You Can Eat

I f you're lucky enough to find yourself in a Croatian home, listen for cries of '*Jedi! Jedi!*' (Eat! Eat!). Sharing food is a big part of the culture, and making sure guests are full and happy is a must. Expect to be offered drinks, snacks, a meal and then second and even third helpings. Tip: don't take too much first time round — it's polite to keep saying, '*da molim*' (yes please)!

Regional Cooking

You'll smell Mediterranean flavours cooking near Croatia's coast. Seafood is the thing to eat here, often grilled, stewed, or in a risotto made with squid ink so it's black. Further inland, get ready to fill up with whopper portions of meat. Cauldron-cooked soups and stews, seasoned with paprika, are popular in the north-east. And don't miss cheesy pastries, called štrukli, around Zagreb.

Croatians love lunch — it's usually the main meal of the day.

Bubbling Under

Ispod čripnje, meaning 'under the lid', is a famous way of cooking throughout Croatia. Chuck all your ingredients (usually lamb, octopus or veal, plus potatoes and herbs) into a pot under a domed iron cover. Place it on hot coals, then pile more coals on top. Leave it — no stirring or checking — to cook in its own juices for at least an hour. When you finally lift the lid, you're in for a treat.

An outdoor kitchen comes in handy when you're cooking *ispod čripnje*!

Special Tastes

Pršut

Paški sir

Kulen

Pršut – a speciality ham, hung to dry in the salty bura wind and served in wafer-thin slices

Paški sir – ewe's cheese from Pag island, where sheep graze on aromatic plants

Kulen – spiced, dried and smoked pork sausage

Janjetina s ražnja – lamb roasted on a spit, often in a roadside car park to tempt passers by

Tartufi (truffles) – rare gourmet mushrooms with a strong flavour; grown underground in Istria, where only specially trained dogs can find them

NO WAY!

Croatia holds the Guinness World Record for the biggest truffle (1.31 kg). Found by Diana the dog in 1999, its estimated value was £3,175!

Tartufi

Festival Fun

Croatia has a crammed calendar of festivals, both traditional and modern. It's a magnet for summer music events, ranging from opera and folk to indie and rock. Locals revel in a stream of religious festivals, and in rural areas people celebrate important times in the farming year. Many Croatian customs are so special that UNESCO has put them on its Intangible Cultural Heritage list.

Annual Carnival Bell Ringers' Pageant

(17 January to Ash Wednesday)

Men from the Kastav region of northwest Croatia parade around wearing sheepskins, masks and bells that ring as they move. The idea is to chase away evil spirits and bring good farming in spring.

INmusic is a modern open-air music festival.

Procession of Queens

(Whitsunday)

Young girls process around the village of Gorjani, half of them dressed as kings and half as queens. The kings dance while the queens sing to the villagers!

Za Krizen

(Thursday before Easter)

Barefoot cross-bearers lead parades around Hvar island for eight hours without resting. At the end, each cross-bearer runs the last 100m to be blessed by his home priest.

You need a good aim for the Sinjska Alka game!

NO WAY!

On the night of 5 December, Croatian children polish their shoes and put them on a windowsill, hoping that St Nicholas will pass by and fill them with treats!

Sinjska Alka

(1st Sunday in August)

At this medieval event in the town of Sinj, horsemen charge at full pelt along a street, aiming lances at an iron ring hung on a rope. Boys here train from a young age to take part.

Feast of St Blaise

(3 February)

This age-old festival celebrates Dubrovnik's patron saint, whose bones are paraded through the town in decorative reliquaries (containers). Hordes of people flood the streets to enjoy a showcase of traditional rituals, crafts, food, songs and dance.

Creative Croatia

Anyone with an arty eye will find something to love in Croatia. There are ancient carvings, medieval murals, modern paintings and traditional crafts. Croatia's buildings are often masterpieces, influenced by Italian and other European styles. In Zagreb you'll find cutting-edge contemporary galleries — there's even a Street Art Museum, with work on walls around the city!

Fancy Lace

Making lace takes skill, and rural women in Croatia have plenty of that! Pag Island is famous for its needlepoint lace, made in a spider's web pattern with geometric designs. Lepoglava's bobbin lace involves braiding threads around spindles, often to make lacy ribbons. On Hvar, Benedictine nuns create aloe lace, weaving threads from the core of fresh aloe leaves!

Traditional lace makes a great souvenir!

Toys n Treats

Toy-making is another centuries-old tradition in Croatia. Wooden toys, from trucks to flutes, are usually hand-carved by men and painted by women. Gingerbread making, or Licitar, has become a handicraft too. Each baker has his or her own style and works within a set area. Hearts are a popular shape to make, decorated with patterns and messages – in edible colours of course!

If someone gives you a licitar with a mirror, it reflects your place in their heart.

Song and Dance

Croatians like to sing in harmony, blending different voices together. In Dalmatia, Klapa is a famous style, where singers stand in a semicircle to perform. Ojkanje is two-part singing with a shaky-voiced sound – the song lasts as long as the lead singer can hold his or her breath! If you prefer to dance in silence, try Nijemo Kolo – it's often performed with no music at all.

A Klapa group sings in Split.

More Information

Websites

- http://www.lonelyplanet.com/croatia
  All you need to prepare for a trip to Croatia.

- http://www.croatia.eu/index.php?lang=2
  Info on everything Croatian, from geography to culture.

- http://croatia.hr/en-GB/Homepage
  The Croatian National Tourist Board site.

- https://www.cia.gov/library/publications/the-world-factbook/geos/hr.html
  The CIA World Factbook Croatia page, with up-to-date info and statistics.

- http://travel.nationalgeographic.com/travel/countries/croatia-facts
  An overview of Croatia, with photographs.

Apps

Google Earth by Google, inc
Explore Croatia (and the rest of the world) from the sky – for free!

Croatia Travel Guide by Triposo
A bundle of background info, city guides, maps and phrasebooks.

Croatia Top 100 for iPhone by imagine Studio Ltd
Few words and lots of pictures showing Croatia's top sights.

Gus on the Go: Croatian for Kids by toojuice, LLC
Join a jet-setting owl to learn the Croatian language! Includes games and animation.

Clips

https://www.youtube.com/watch?v=bQiFB7OfPWc
A slideshow of Croatia's World Heritage Sites.

https://www.youtube.com/watch?v=EWXH182TpPk
The Sinjista Alka horse-riding festival in action.

https://www.youtube.com/watch?v=GivAc77gJgg
The Annual Carnival Bell Ringers Pageant.

https://www.youtube.com/watch?v=fjm9QXUVYLA
A demonstration of Ojkanje singing.

https://www.youtube.com/watch?v=sciwtWcfdH4
Learn about Klapa multi-part singing.

https://www.youtube.com/watch?v=69LOMscp5QU
All about the Nijemo Kolo dance.

https://www.youtube.com/watch?v=JuMHTNeUDri
Watch Croatian lace being made.

Books

Lonely Planet Croatia
(Lonely Planet, 2015)

Berlitz: Croatia Pocket Guide
(Berlitz Travel, 2014)

DK Eyewitness Top 10 Travel Guide: Dubrovnik & the Dalmatian Coast
(Dorling Kindersley, 2014)

Insight Guides: Croatia
(Insight, 2014)

Croatia isn't called Croatia in Croatian! Their word for it is Hrvatska – that's why Croatian websites end in '.hr'.

Television

Two episodes of *Doctor Who* – *The Vampires of Venice* and *Vincent and the Doctor* – starring Matt Smith as the Doctor, were filmed in Trogir, Croatia in 2010.

Glossary

agritourism Tourism at a farm or ranch.

aloe A type of plant with very thick leaves.

communist Following a system where all property and industry is owned by the community, rather than individuals.

empire A group of countries ruled over by a single monarch (usually a king, queen or emperor).

ethnic cleansing The mass removal or killing of an ethnic or religious group from a certain area.

European Union (EU) A group of European countries whose governments work together economically and politically.

kingdom A territory ruled by a king or queen.

maritime To do with the sea.

republic A state where power is held by the people, with an elected president rather than a monarch.

rural Relating to the countryside, rather than towns.

sphinx A stone figure with a lion's body and (usually) a human head.

stalactite An icicle-like formation that hangs from the roof of a cave.

stalagmite A column rising from the floor of a cave.

Index